THE INSISTENCE OF HARM

Contemporary Spanish-Language Poetry in Translation

UNIVERSITY PRESS OF FLORIDA

Florida A&M University, Tallahassee
Florida Atlantic University, Boca Raton
Florida Gulf Coast University, Ft. Myers
Florida International University, Miami
Florida State University, Tallahassee
New College of Florida, Sarasota
University of Central Florida, Orlando
University of Florida, Gainesville
University of North Florida, Jacksonville
University of South Florida, Tampa
University of West Florida, Pensacola

Contemporary Spanish-Language Poetry in Translation series
sponsored by the University of West Florida

UNIVERSITY PRESS OF FLORIDA
Gainesville · Tallahassee · Tampa · Boca Raton
Pensacola · Orlando · Miami · Jacksonville · Ft. Myers · Sarasota

THE
INSISTENCE
OF HARM

Fernando Valverde

Translated by Allen Josephs and Laura Juliet Wood

Publication of this book has been aided by a grant from the University of West Florida.

This book may be available in an electronic edition.

Originally published by VISOR LIBROS, MADRID, 2014, as *La insistencia del daño*

24 23 22 21 20 19   6 5 4 3 2 1

Library of Congress Control Number: 2019931198
ISBN 978-0-8130-6435-2

The University Press of Florida is the scholarly publishing agency for the State
University System of Florida, comprising Florida A&M University, Florida Atlantic
University, Florida Gulf Coast University, Florida International University, Florida
State University, New College of Florida, University of Central Florida, University of
Florida, University of North Florida, University of South Florida, and University of
West Florida.

University Press of Florida
2046 NE Waldo Road
Suite 2100
Gainesville, FL 32609
http://upress.ufl.edu

Contents

INTRODUCTION

IN 2014, PROFESSOR REMEDIOS GARCÍA SÁNCHEZ of the University of Granada sent a survey to critics and professors of Hispanic literature, asking them to name the best Spanish-language poets born since 1970. Of the specialists solicited, 197 responded, representing 103 universities worldwide, with Harvard, Princeton, Columbia, Oxford, and Bologna leading the list. Fernando Valverde garnered the most votes: number one young poet in the Spanish language, which has a potential readership of 560 million people.

Spanish poetry is the earliest poetry among the romance languages. *Jarchas,* two-line endings to Arabic and Jewish amorous poems, written in early Spanish, date from the tenth century, at the height of the power of Muslim Spain. Poets recited them to public acclaim in the squares of Córdoba, Sevilla, and Granada.

The poetry of the most brilliant period, the Spanish Golden Age, included writers such as Miguel de Cervantes, Lope de Vega, Luis de Góngora, Francisco de Quevedo, San Juan de la Cruz, and Mexican poet Sor Juana Inés de la Cruz. The Golden Age lasted from the late fifteenth to the late seventeenth centuries and paralleled an equally important period in English poetry. In the late seventeenth century, Spanish poetry fell into a period of lesser brilliance until 1898, when the Generations of 1898 and 1927, together with Rubén Darío's Modernismo movement, rekindled the poetic ardor and originality of Spain and Latin America. Juan Ramón Jiménez and Vicente Aleixandre, representatives of the two generations, won Nobel Prizes in

Literature in 1956 and 1977, as did Chilean poets Gabriela Mistral and Pablo Neruda in 1945 and 1971.

After the Spanish Civil War (1936–1939), the so-called social poets such as Angel González evaded and mocked Franco's censorship. This legacy of subtle satire continued into the post-Franco period in the writing of poets such as Luis García Montero and Benjamín Prado. These poets in turn encouraged a new generation of contemporary poets practicing what has become known as the Poetry of Uncertainty, the group being led by Fernando Valverde. We might think of Fernando Valverde as the leader of a group of poets of *ontological* uncertainty, as we will see below.

It is possible we are now in a new period of great Spanish poetry, a twenty-first century extension of the poetic period of the 1920s and 1930s, interrupted by the Spanish Civil War, the consequences of which still haunt Spain. The war and Franco's dictatorship have protracted what is in fact a poetic moment—or movement—that began as early as 1898 and continues unabated today. We see this extended period as an unbroken—but stuttering—path from Antonio Machado to Fernando Valverde and his group via Lorca, Angel González, and many others.

Spanish poetry has often proceeded in groups, frequently referred to as generations. The Poetry of Uncertainty is in no small measure Fernando Valverde's creation. This group of young poets is unusual in that it has no national or geographic boundaries—rather, it is intentionally transatlantic, actively breaking down borders and nationalities. Its only limitation is the multifarious Spanish tongue, and its growing membership comes from Spain, Mexico, El Salvador, Nicaragua, Colombia, Bolivia, Chile, and Argentina.

There is a historical precedent in the great Nicaraguan poet Rubén Darío and his Modernista group, which brought together Latin American and Spanish poets at the turn of the twentieth century. However, the Poetry of Uncertainty is different in a fundamental way. These poets are in constant contact with each other through the internet and via social media. They travel extensively, collaborating in international poetry festivals, forming a cohesive unit materially impossible in Rubén Darío's day, an expanding pluralistic group virtually without precedent. Fernando Valverde is currently their leading voice, one we are delighted to bring to English-language readers in this volume.

Here are some excerpts from a recent conversation we had with Fernando Valverde about his early life and influences:

All the memories of my childhood are of my grandparents and my mother. Especially in the summer, in a Mediterranean pueblo called Almuñécar, which was originally the Phoenician town of Sexi, settled nearly 3,000 years ago. My poetry is full of that place. We had an apartment facing the sea and for me it was paradise. Later we sold it and that ruined everything. The marine landscape in my poetry is usually an allusion to that happiness of my childhood.

My parents divorced when I was twelve. I have two brothers, one two years younger and the other five. My mother raised us by painting pictures and furniture. We were not the best of boys. I still feel guilty about that. When I was old enough to help, she got sick. I always admired the women of my family. They taught me art, my mother as a painter and my grandmother as a reader of literature. They were my points of reference and were victims of a very male-dominated society.

When my parents separated, I went to live with my grandparents. I began writing thanks to my grandmother, who had a large library. It was a mysterious place and it fascinated me. The first book I read was *The Inferno*—a strange choice, perhaps, but I was fascinated by Hell. After that I read *Les Miserables* by Victor Hugo. The first poet who attracted me was Pablo Neruda—his love poems, of course. Then Federico. That's where I spent my adolescence, inside my grandmother's library. Even before [that], I practically lived with my grandparents. Just me. It was where I wanted to be. My mother and brothers were two blocks away.

I am from Granada, as you well know. So I have always been under the shadow of Lorca. Aside from the summers in Almuñécar, the landscape of Granada was the landscape of my life, and it is a fratricidal city: Beautiful and terrible. Where if you stand out, you are rewarded with the hatred of everyone else.

I left because it was a place that terrified me. The worst bourgeoisie of Europe, as Lorca called it in his last interview, continues to stir things up. It has not changed.

Fernando began writing poetry in his teens and published his first collection, *Favorable Wind*, in 2002. In 2003, Fernando and fellow poet Daniel Rodríguez Moya founded the FIP, the Festival Internacional de Poesía (International Poetry Festival), which has become in the intervening years one of the finest poetry festivals in the world. The FIP has invited innumerable Spanish-language poets, as well as international poets such as Yevgeny Yevtushenko, Yusef Komunyakaa, Richard Blanco, Paul Muldoon, Carolyn Forché, Natasha Trethewey, and novelist and Nobel laureate J. M. Coetzee to Granada to read from their works.

In 2004, Valverde published his next collection, *Reasons to Flee a Cold City*, in which cities in winter, Granada among others, return him to the intense nostalgia of his childhood summers on the Mediterranean. This second book marks his early entry into Visor, perhaps the Hispanic world's most prestigious poetry house.

In 2010, Valverde's mother suffered an irreparable cerebral hemorrhage that, in his words from the preface to *Poesía (1997–2017)*, his collected poems, "stole forever most of her memories." Using the image of the pelican's drop and consequent blindness (pelicans make long, repeated dives into the water to catch fish, which damages their eyes), he wrote *The Eyes of the Pelican*, his third collection, drawing on his mother's story as an example of how dreams crash over and again into darkest reality. The book, published in Spain first, won the Emilio Alarcos prize and was then published in Argentina, Mexico, Colombia, and the United States (translated by Gordon E. McNeer). From the book's first poem, "The Fall," here is one brief example of a tragedy that will remain with him:

Leave aside your flesh,
you have beaten your face against the water so much
that the light has broken.

It was around this time that Valverde—collaborating with Spanish poet Raquel Lanseros (second on that list of the greatest Spanish-language poets born since 1970, although there was no list then), Jorge

Galán from El Salvador (third), Alí Calderón from Mexico (fifth), and Federico Díaz-Granados from Colombia (seventh)—began forming the Poetry of Uncertainty. It is not coincidence that five of the top seven poets on the list ranked by 197 critics and specialists form the nucleus of this extraordinarily talented group. Fernando Valverde is not only an accomplished poet, he is also an entrepreneur of poetry.

In 2014, Valverde was nominated for a Grammy Award for a record he made with singer Juan Pinilla that fused flamenco music and his poetry. In 2014 Valverde also published the book we have translated here, *The Insistence of Harm*, which was named Book of the Year by the Latin American Writers Institute at New York University. It continues the theme of his mother's misfortune but now combines it with the loss of love to create a powerful current of loss as a theme made manifest from the title onward. The collection is a series of poignant lyric poems ranging in scope and location from India to the Balkans to Spain and to Latin America and encompassing *harm* in its various guises, from war to disease to heartbreak to suicide.

In the first lines of the poem "Harm," we learn that there is no defense against harm:

> We found out afterwards,
> no time for anything

And in "The Earthquake" the poet tells us:

> We will not be safe until we are dead.
> Maybe pain pursues us after all
> like mud stuck to our shoes.

In "Becoming Shadow," loneliness is overwhelming:

> You are turning into shadow
> and touch my eyes
> the way the blind touch air when they look,
> and you cross the morass
> to your room
> at the least opportune moment
> leaving things in silence
> to become the solitude
> that possesses me.

These poems speak to a diverse world of readers of poetry—their poignancy, accessibility, and open emotion are universal. In the first paragraph of the introduction to *Poesía ante la incertidumbre*, the anthology of the Uncertainty group, Valverde's group defines the scope of the ontological uncertainty that plagues all of us, beginning with these words: "The historical moment we have been dealt is marked by uncertainty in every sense of the word." They go on to explain that "Uncertainty seems to take in everything: politics, morality, economics, the new forms of communication that paradoxically have brought about a greater lack of communication. . . . Also, the old utopias that once seemed attainable and filled millions with hope have crumbled . . . adding even more uncertainty to everything that surrounds us."

His group writes that poetry is the positive act of confronting uncertainty with a poem that sheds some light on reality, adding "If a poem does not make sense, what is usually happening is that the poet has not done the job right." They allude to rival groups of poets without specifically mentioning them by name—the *novísimos* and the poets of silence—whom they take to task for their intentional obscurity, citing a poem by Angel González (1925–2008), whose memory and poetry are the guiding inspiration for the group:

> Tears filled the eyes of the reader
> and a loving voice whispered in his ear:
> "Why are you crying, if everything in that book is a lie?"
> And he replied: "I know;
> but what I feel is the truth."

In response, the group writes, "This poem by Angel González sums up exceptionally well what we understand as the miracle of poetry, the capacity to transmit feeling thanks to language and to the different resources the genre offers. Without the attempt to transmit emotions, to fill the void, to reflect on the world, to become a thousand voices—the poem is hollow, it has no life." Poetry, then—as Valverde and his contemporaries in the Uncertainty group understand it—may be the best recourse in dealing with our uncertainty.

The prologue goes on to offer a description of poetry: "Poetry has belonged and will always belong to all of humanity; it is a clear and luminous kaleidoscope that enters the deepest recesses of our awareness." It is born of a poetic "I" but always pools into "we." While not using the word "archetype," the group is clearly seeking universality, and astutely mentions British poet Robert Graves, who held that a true poem made one's hair stand on end because it invokes the White Goddess, the archetypal core we all carry within. The Uncertainty group also believes that poetry must "confront power"—any power that causes the loss of dialogue and that invites silence. They finish by returning to Graves: "We want to say goodbye to all that." Cleverly and wisely they synthesize social concern and the deepest well of our existence. This combination is the group's hallmark, and it is everywhere evident in *The Insistence of Harm.*

Most recently, Valverde published *Poesía (1997–2017)* with Visor, a compilation of his earlier volumes. In the prologue, he writes that "Poetry is one of the few possible forms to establish a link between the real and the extraordinary. To achieve that, the poet needs to lean on two worlds with the certainty of a bridge." Then he tells us that the poet's task is not to raise an architectural monument, but to find "a path that we can traverse, some habitable place. For me the poem has never been an end in itself, but rather a way for emotion to flow." And he concludes, "If poetry can contribute to a better world, it is because it helps us understand the pain of others."

In the final paragraph, speaking of the journey of life and poetry, Valverde echoes Dante and numerous Spanish poets—Gustavo Adolfo Becquer, Juan Ramón Jiménez, Antonio Machado, and Federico García Lorca come instantly to mind—when he says: "In the midst of that journey, between the light of the world and its shadows, between beauty and pain, there was poetry. I could only reach her a few times, but when she brushed against me it was like a miracle. Since then I have done nothing but pursue her, always with the fear that she might abandon me forever." *The Insistence of Harm* proves such fears unfounded, and it brings a new and important poetic voice to English-language readers.

Fernando Valverde's poetry has been translated into numerous languages and has earned many prestigious awards, including the Federico García Lorca Prize, the Juan Ramón Jiménez, the Emilio Alarcos, and others. For a decade he was a correspondent for *El País*, sending dispatches from the Balkans and the Middle East. He holds a doctorate in Hispanic Philology from the University of Granada and currently teaches at the University of Virginia.

We consider Fernando Valverde to be one of the best living poets writing in Spanish today, so we were pleased when he asked us to translate *La insistencia del daño*, now *The Insistence of Harm*. He richly deserves this translation into English.

A note about translation: This series, Contemporary Spanish-Language Poetry in Translation, seeks to present a group of contemporary Spanish-language poets in a bilingual format accessible to students of Spanish and lay readers alike. The translations are as faithful to the original as possible in order to facilitate comprehension and retain meaning.

Allen Josephs and Laura Juliet Wood

Pensacola, San Miguel de Allende, and Nerja

THE INSISTENCE OF HARM

Cruces y sombras

CROSSES AND SHADOWS

1

LA JOVEN DE SCARBOROUGH

(Ana Brontë, 1820–1849)

Ana mira el desierto,
una tormenta espesa de nieve sobre el mar,
piensa en su tos, en la sangre que escupe
que pertenece a ella como el hambre o la fiebre.

Sus pulmones se extinguen,
es 1849
y ha llegado hasta Scarborough
huyendo de la muerte.
Va a respirar el mar,
el verde de las algas que agoniza en la arena.

Siente el agua y la espuma
y un sudor que le sube hasta la boca
como si fuera aceite.

Se asoma a la ventana,
inhala las agujas que le quedan al sol
y el olor de la tarde le recuerda al pescado
pero también al paso de los días.

El blanco de su cuerpo en el abismo
es amor y es deseo,
el vuelo de los pájaros
y también su caída.

Alguien la ve pasar,
atraviesa el invierno más de un siglo después,
delgada como niebla,
viento detrás de las cortinas
o una mano de hielo que dibuja un cristal
de párpados cerrados.

THE MAID OF SCARBOROUGH

(Anne Brontë, 1820–1849)

Anne gazes at empty space
a thick snowstorm over the sea,
she thinks about her cough, the blood she spits
that belongs to her like hunger or fever.

Her lungs are failing,
it's 1849
and she has come to Scarborough
fleeing death.
She's going to breathe the sea,
the green of algae rotting on sand.

She feels the water and foam
and a sweat rising into her throat
like oil.

She leans into the window,
inhaling the final needles of fading sunlight
and the odor of the afternoon reminds her of fish
and, also, the passing of days.

Her body white in the abyss
is love is desire,
the flight of birds
and also their fall.

Someone sees her pass,
she traverses winter more than a century later,
thin as mist,
wind behind the curtains
or an icy hand tracing on the windowpane
through closed eyes.

La alegría hecha escombros.

Ahora está maldita,
se cierran las ventanas a su paso,
se marchitan las flores y el mundo es un desierto,
una tormenta espesa que sube hasta la boca.

Joy turned to ruin.

Now she is cursed,
windows close when she passes,
flowers wilt and the world is empty space,
a thick storm rising into the throat.

RATKO MLADIĆ CONVERSA CON LA MUERTE

A Nieves

Ratko Mladić intuye que cada acantilado
es el miedo y el vértigo,
es la oportunidad
que atraviesa los puentes
con los ojos clavados en el suelo.

Él lo sabe y procura
derribar cada puente.

Luego piensa en su hija,
en el aire tomado por las conversaciones
y el sonido que tuvo la rabia en un disparo
hueco como el silencio,
como quedan los labios
delante de una frase suspendida.

Ratko Mladić lo sabe,
ha conversado mucho con la muerte,
largas noches en vela que le dan un sentido
al temor que acomodan las miradas
como ropa inservible.

Piensa en su casa ardiendo,
en el modo en que el fuego doblega cuanto toca,
ceniza en las palabras,
madera que es carbón y que un día fue el aire.

Todos lo ven pasar,
todos vierten su miedo sobre él.
Él ahora es el miedo
y siente sus certezas y la seguridad
de quien está del lado de la muerte.

RATKO MLADIĆ TALKS WITH DEATH

For Nieves

Ratko Mladić intuits every precipice
as fear, as vertigo,
as opportunity
crossing bridges
with its eyes nailed to the ground.

He knows and tries
to demolish each bridge.

Then he thinks of his daughter,
of breath spent in conversation
and the sound of rage in a single shot
hollow like silence
like lips
suspended in mid-phrase.

Ratko Mladić knows,
has spoken often with death,
long sleepless nights that explain
the fear that faces wear
like useless clothing.

He thinks about his house burning,
how fire doubles over everything it touches,
ashes in the words,
wood that is coal that once was air.

Everyone watches him go by,
everyone empties into him their fear.
Now he is fear itself
and feels his certainties and the security
of one who is on death's side.

Ratko Mladić se aleja de los vivos.
Un cerdo degollado preside su figura
en el hotel Fontana.
Se siente un general,
habla como el destino de los hombres.
—*Dios no puede ayudaros.*

Dos soldados conducen a un anciano a una casa,
un disparo separa el cuerpo de la vida
como separa a un hombre de sus asesinos.

Toda la muerte pasa en pocas horas.
Ratko Mladić despierta
unos minutos antes de la madrugada
y sale a caminar por las calles de Bratunac.
Puede mirar al cielo,
también puede rezar pero prefiere
el silencio profundo que ocupa el universo
a la vuelta del grito,
su paz indescriptible,
el olor de la sangre
que convierte en metálico el aspecto del lodo.

Ratko Mladić lo sabe,
mira el amanecer,
el sol viene del este y llega puntual.

Ratko Mladić detesta las impuntualidades,
la muerte es siempre pronto.

Ahora que son más leves sus conversaciones
y que su voz se encoge
y el aliento entorpece las palabras

Ratklo Mladić stays away from the living.
A boar's head resides above his figure
at the Hotel Fontana.
He thinks of himself as a general
and speaks as though he were man's destiny.
"God cannot help you."

Two soldiers lead an old man to a house,
a shot separates the body from life
as it separates a man from his assassins.

All this death takes only a few hours.
Ratko Mladić wakes
minutes before dawn
and goes out to walk the streets of Bratunak.
He can look up at heaven
and pray but he prefers
the deep silence filling the universe
after the scream,
indescribable peace,
the smell of blood
that turns mud metallic.

Ratko Mladić knows
and watches it dawn,
the sun comes from the east and arrives punctually.

Ratko Mladić detests lack of punctuality,
death is always on time.

Now that his conversations are lighter
his voice shrinks
and his breath dulls his words

igual que la metralla
o los campos minados
o las pruebas que pesan en su contra . . .

Ratko Mladić ya sabe
que tampoco la muerte va a respetarle a él,
fiel domador de ejércitos,
general de sus sombras.

like a machine gun
or minefields
or evidence weighed against him . . .

Ratko Mladić now knows
death will not respect him either,
faithful trainer of armies,
general of their shadows.

CAMINANTE SOBRE UN MAR DE NIEBLA

El caminante intuye la caída,
siente el vértigo,
piensa que no hay final que no sea el origen
de todo cuanto fluye.

Las olas son montañas que crecen como angustia.

La roca que se adentra en el abismo
lo separa de todo lo que no sucedió.
Las cosas que pudieron quedarse en el pasado
llegan ahora, increpan con sus dudas,
son niebla que no deja ver la niebla.

El caminante teme
el salto que sucede a los fracasos,
pero queda un desorden tras sus hombros,
un hastío de lluvia que ocurre en otro tiempo.

WALKER ON A SEA OF FOG

The walker intuits the fall,
senses the vertigo,
thinks there's no end that is not the beginning
of everything that flows.

The waves are mountains growing like nausea.

The rock entering deep into the abyss
separates him from all that did not happen.
Things that could have stayed in the past
come back now, rebuking him with doubt,
fog that won't let him see the fog.

The walker fears
the leap that follows failure,
but a wreck remains lodged between his shoulders,
a tedium of rain falling in another time.

LLANTO DE DIFUNTOS

En memoria de Francisco Ruiz Udiel

Ahora que puedo ver tu soledad
comprendo el equilibrio de las piedras,
tu paso lento por las avenidas
y la prisa en la tarde
cruza los soportales.

Pasa tu soledad por las calles de Pátzcuaro,
sostiene las estatuas
sobre tiempo dormido.
La vida que sucede en los susurros,
que se aparta en voz baja,
evita el desenlace que persiguen tus pies.

Los alacranes tienen
afiladas sus pinzas y el veneno
es tiempo vulnerable,
tierra en el empedrado,
esperanzas tendidas junto al fuego
o escarcha inoportuna.

Es todo cuanto debes.

Esta lluvia de pájaros
que destrozan sus huesos contra el suelo
sucede en tus poemas.

Yo sé que no es posible.

Vimos tu soledad como una casa en ruinas,
pendiente del aviso de los desprendimientos.

LAMENT FOR THE DEAD

In memory of Francisco Ruiz Udiel

Now that I can see your loneliness
I understand the equilibrium of these stones,
in your slow passage along the avenue
through the bustle of afternoon
you cross beneath the archways.

You travel the streets of Pátzcuaro,
your solitude sustaining the statues
asleep in time.
The life that happens in murmurs,
that steps aside in a hushed voice,
avoids the unraveling plot your feet pursue.

The scorpions have
sharpened their claws and their venom
is vulnerable time,
dirt on the cobblestones,
hopes laid next to the fire
or untimely frost.

It's everything you owe.

This rain of birds
snapping their bones on the ground
happens in your poems.

I know it is not possible.

We saw your loneliness like a ruined house,
waiting for the sounds of collapse.

No sé si ese eras tú
o una parte de ti
que la muerte no había invitado a su cena.

I don't know if that was you
or some part of you
that death had not invited to her banquet.

CON LOS OJOS ABIERTOS CAMINAS
POR LA MUERTE

Para Alí Calderón
que me acompañó a la última quebrada

En la última quebrada de los Andes,
donde la cordillera se hace piedras
que llenan los caminos
y caen como nevadas,
donde pastan el hambre y la pobreza
y en las gasolineras
hay una calma muda que se apoya en el aire.

Alguien se llama Ernesto,
alguien dice tu nombre en el mercado,
o en caminos de tierra que atraviesan los niños
que comen los insectos,
que se beben la sangre de los niños
y dejan en las puertas la marca de la altura
y unos viejos zapatos
sobre el tendido eléctrico
y unos viejos zapatos en los pies del que cruza
el ultimo desierto de los Andes,
un valle en el dolor,
las piedras rotas que caen como tormentas
sobre esta soledad de cuerpos apagados
que lleva siempre hasta los hospitales.

Dicen que eres un muerto de los que nunca mueren,
que tus ojos mirando hacia el vacío
se han clavado en el techo del Hospital de Malta
que hoy ocupan el dengue y la tuberculosis,
que pastan en la hierba
como animales pobres y delgados

WITH OPEN EYES YOU WALK
THROUGH DEATH

For Alí Calderón,
who came with me to the last ravine

In the last ravine of the Andes
the cordillera turns to rocks
that fill the roads
and fall like snowstorms,
hunger and poverty graze
and in gas stations
a mute calm hangs in the air.

Someone is named Ernesto,
someone says your name in the market,
or on dirt roads where children cross
eating insects
that drink the children's blood,
who leave in doorways marks of their height
and old shoes
on a power line
and old shoes on the feet of one crossing
the last desert of the Andes,
a valley in grief,
broken stones falling like thunderstorms
on the solitude of burnt-out bodies
that always end up in the hospital.

They say you are one of the dead that never die,
that your eyes staring into space
are fixed on the ceiling of the Hospital de Malta
occupied today by dengue and tuberculosis
that graze in the grass
like poor skinny animals

que beben en los charcos
o se tragan el plástico de los contenedores.

Como la tierra de los cementerios,
nada puede callarte,
con los ojos abiertos caminas por la muerte,
alguien repite Ernesto,
ya se marcha la lluvia hacia otro lado,
alguien siente las piernas
pesadas como el plomo
y acaba en una cama del Hospital de Malta,
una tarde de junio,
ya ha terminado octubre,
van a matar a un hombre,
no cruzan los pasillos con su paso de fieras,
no se escucha la huella de las botas
como en aquella tarde
de mil novecientos sesenta y siete
que fue la tierra para los cementerios
y los ojos abiertos la esperaron
en la lavandería
al otro lado de las cordilleras.

Ahora siente un dolor de sangre en los tendones,
ha pasado la fiebre,
ha cruzado la muerte hacia otra cama,
se ha instalado en el gas que llega a la cocina
o ha puesto ya sus huevos en las pinzas
o sobre la destreza en los quirófanos.

Sucede así en el valle,
con lógica de hambre y la costumbre
de ver caer las piedras.

that drink from puddles
or gulp down pieces of plastic containers.

Like dirt from cemeteries,
nothing can silence you,
with open eyes you walk through death,
again someone says Ernesto,
the rain shifts somewhere else,
someone feels his legs
heavy as lead
and is carried to a bed in the Hospital de Malta,
one June afternoon,
October gone now,
they're going to kill a man,
they don't cross the halls with wild steps,
you don't hear the sound of boots
like that other afternoon
in nineteen sixty-seven
that was dirt for cemeteries
and open eyes waited for death
in the laundry
on the other side of the cordillera.

Now he feels a blood-pain in his tendons,
the fever is gone,
death has crossed toward another bed,
has nestled herself in the gas entering the kitchen
or has already laid eggs on tongs
or upon the surgical skills of doctors in the operating room.

That's how it happens in the valley,
with the logic of hunger and the habit
of watching rocks fall.

En las últimas horas de esta tarde de junio,
el muchacho que tiene
la sangre coagulada en las rodillas
se atropella en la hierba,
no hay ruido de helicópteros,
sólo dos extranjeros entran al hospital
pero hay en sus gargantas una rabia durmiente
que no altera el silencio
de la lavandería.

Ellos van a volver a Santa Cruz,
pero el joven que arrastra
la pierna y las rodillas
ha nacido en el Valle,
y ha visto que la muerte cruzaba el hospital
y hasta la calle Sucre
y la ha visto escondida en una madriguera de culebras
o en el agua estancada.

Él sabe que a la muerte no se entra
con los ojos abiertos,
tal vez porque sospecha
que no hay nada que ver,
alguien le dijo un día
que la ceguera es blanca,
será la oscuridad de cualquier modo
y no hay nada que ver,
y los ojos abiertos perdidos al vacío
siguen clavados en el techo
de la lavandería
mirando a algún lugar,

In the late hours of this afternoon in June,
the boy who has
clotted blood on his knees
rushes headlong through grass,
there's no noise of helicopters,
only two foreigners entering the hospital
but in their throats there's a dormant rage
that does not alter the silence
in the laundry.

They will return to Santa Cruz,
but the youth who drags
his leg and his knees
was born in Valle,
and has seen death cross through the hospital
and out to Calle Sucre
and he saw her hidden in a den of snakes
and in stagnant water.

He knows you don't go into death
with open eyes,
maybe because he suspects
there's nothing to see,
someone told him one day
that blindness is white,
it will be darkness anyway
and there will be nothing to see,
and open eyes lost in the void
still fixed on the ceiling
in the laundry
looking at some place,

señalando un camino o sosteniendo
alguna dirección,
allí donde se rompen cordilleras
y las piedras se clavan en los ojos
y destrozan los huesos de los campesinos,
allí fuiste a morir,
a la ceguera blanca,
traiciones que recorren las calles como cables,
alguien te llama Ernesto en el mercado
o en las gasolineras,
un joven atraviesa la hierba en una silla,
ahora dice tu nombre
como quien busca alivio en medio del dolor,
allí fuiste a morir
con los ojos abiertos.

pointing out a road or holding
some course,
there where cordilleras collide
and rocks nail you in the eyes
and destroy the bones of the *campesinos*,
that's where you went to die,
in the white blindness,
treacheries lining the streets like wires,
someone calls you Ernesto in the market
or in the gas stations,
a youth crosses the grass in a wheelchair,
now he says your name
like someone in the midst of pain seeking relief,
that's where you went to die
with your eyes open.

IZET SARAJLIĆ CRUZA UNA PUERTA
QUE CONDUCE AL DOLOR

Vlado sale a buscar su bala cada tarde.
Cuando sus fuerzas fallan,
deshace su camino para volver a casa,
si es que existe la casa o siquiera un camino.

En Ilidža un estanque es un embudo,
la corriente que lleva a Sarajevo,
que atraviesa los túneles,
rodea el aeropuerto,
y un sonido de aviones dibuja otro país,
también una frontera
que separa el invierno de la lluvia.

Izet Sarajlić mira la forma en que la lluvia
es una puerta abierta hacia el dolor,
el recuerdo de un nombre o de un jardín,
una ventana al este que un día fue una casa.

Vlado regresa de su caminata,
muy pocos lo saludan,
su tristeza se ha vuelto contagiosa
y nadie tiene ya palabras para él,
tan poco lo separa de los muertos
que ni él mismo se habla.

El rastro de un misil corta el silencio,
y tampoco era el suyo.

Mientras, en las colinas,
los francotiradores
van a ser la destreza de la muerte,
un silbido que rompa los cristales,

IZET SARAJLIĆ CROSSES A THRESHOLD
LEADING TO GRIEF

Vlado goes looking for his bullet every afternoon.
When his strength fails
he walks home the way he came,
if there is a home or a road even.

In Ilidža a pond is a funnel,
the current that flows toward Sarajevo,
that courses through tunnels,
skirts the airport,
and the sound of aircraft paints the image of another country,
and also a border
that separates winter from rain.

Izet Sarajlić watches how rain
is a door open to grief,
the memory of a name or a garden,
a window looking east that once was a house.

Vlado returns from his walk,
very few greet him,
his sadness has become contagious
and no one speaks,
so little separates him from the dead
that not even he talks to himself.

The trail of a missile slices the silence,
but it's not his either.

Meanwhile, up in the hills,
snipers
will become skillful agents of death,
a whistling that breaks windows,

un balcón al vacío.

Izet Sarajlić mira su reloj,
no hay respuesta a la espera,
después sigue la línea del tranvía,
el número catorce,
sube hasta el cementerio del león,
en la calle la gente regresa del mercado
y corre con sus bolsas cuando se acerca el cruce
más silencioso y sordo.

Izet Sarajlić mira hacia ambos lados
y su paso incesante es ya necesidad
de volver al amor
mientras su rostro absorbe la impaciencia
del frío en los zapatos.

Él sabe que está muerto,
nadie conoce aquello que le hace sufrir.

a balcony on the abyss.

Izet Sarajlić looks at his watch,
there is no response to waiting,
then he follows the trolley line,
number fourteen,
and climbs to the Lion Cemetery,
on the street people are returning from market
and run with their bags as the crossroad draws near
more silent and deaf.

Izet Sarajlić looks both ways
and his incessant step is now the need
to return to love
as his face reflects the impatience
of his cold shoes.

He knows he's dead,
no one knows what makes him suffer.

LA TIERRA DE LOS DÉBILES

Llegaron como plagas para arrasarlo todo,
se llevaron lo poco que guardaba en las manos
después de ver entrar la muerte en casa
sin saber quién sería el elegido.

Y trajeron el daño,
el fruto del sudor y de las horas blancas
que fueron la renuncia del futuro
y su nostalgia sucia que manchaba la ropa
y dejaba un aspecto de tristeza,
de fiesta suspendida.

Ella estaba mirando
aquel atardecer que se bebió la luz,
toda la luz que pudo.

Ahora sigue un rastro sobre sus propias huellas
que conducen a otro.

LAND OF THE WEAK

They arrived like plagues and leveled everything,
they took what little she held in her hands
as she watched death enter her house
not knowing who would be taken.

And they brought harm,
the fruit of labor and of white hours,
the renunciation of the future,
and the filthy nostalgia that stained their clothes,
and left an aspect of sadness,
of a celebration brought to an end.

She was watching
that dusk that drank the light,
all the light it could.

Now she follows a trail back over her own tracks
leading to another.

El viaje
del mundo

No lo sabíamos: nacemos ya mordidos,
hermana, por la muerte

PIEDAD BONNETT

VOYAGE OF THE WORLD

We didn't know: we were born, sister, already bitten by death.

PIEDAD BONNETT

2

CELIA

Nacida hoy

No conoces la lluvia ni los árboles,
pero ya eres un bosque.

Hoy que comienza el mundo para ti,
que se pueblan tus ojos con el mar,
que todos te reciben como en una estación
donde se espera siempre,
que es principio y asombro,
mapas que no aseguran un lugar donde ir.

Hoy que el mundo comienza,
tristeza inadvertida,
eres el tiempo limpio,
el olor a madera y el silencio,
las preguntas sin sombras
y el amor sin orgullo del que ha perdido todo.

Es esa mi certeza,
las olas, el océano,
tu risa que es un pájaro.

Has traído el murmullo de un recuerdo,
los pies pequeños, como pequeño
es el rastro de nieve que has dejado
en las horas de enero.

Cómo será la vida cuando crezca en tus manos
con la fragilidad de las buenas noticias,
como un pez que se escurre para volver al río.

Una tarde cualquiera,
con la misma sorpresa que un amor,

CELIA

Born today

You know neither the rain nor the trees,
yet you're already a forest.

Now the world begins for you,
now your eyes fill with the sea,
now everyone receives you as in some station
where one waits forever,
beginning and surprise,
maps promising no place to go.

Today the world begins,
unforeseen gloom,
you are limpid time,
the scent of wood and silence,
questions without shadows
and love without the pride of one who has lost everything.

This is my certainty,
waves, the ocean,
your laughter is a bird.

You've brought the murmur of a memory,
little feet, small like
the trace of snow you left
in the January hours.

How life will be growing in your hands
with the fragility of good news,
like a fish wriggling back to the river.

On any given afternoon,
with a surprise like falling in love,

vas a sentir la brisa que ha tocado los árboles
con su cansancio antiguo.

Hay veces que es rugosa y escuece como un fósforo
cuando enciende un recuerdo . . .

Tus manos brillan,
no hay sombras ni puñales,
puedo ver los cometas
arañando la noche
como un barco que zarpa y se adentra en la niebla.

La vida es una casa donde habita un extraño,
un jardín del pasado al que no volverás,
una orilla que buscas con miedo a los fantasmas.

Pero también la vida
es una luz detrás de una ventana
cuando la oscuridad
ocupa cada hueco y cada continente.

Esta noche es oscura,
el tren busca unos brazos
que están al otro lado de las horas.

Mientras, pienso en el modo de decirte
que los sueños son parte de nosotros
como un embarcadero es un viaje.

Porque ya eres un bosque,
y hay delfines, y lagos, y montañas,
y amores imposibles
que se llamarán Celia.

you're going to feel the breeze that has touched the trees
with its ancient weariness.

There are times when it's rough and it stings like a match
lighting up a memory . . .

Your hands shine,
no shadows, no daggers,
I can see shooting stars
tearing through the night
like a ship setting sail into fog.

Life is a house where a stranger lives,
a garden from the past where you'll never return,
a shore you seek, afraid of ghosts.

Yet life is also
a light in the window
when darkness
fills every hollow and every continent.

This night is dark,
the train seeks arms
on the other side of time.

Meanwhile, I'm trying to tell you
that dreams are part of us
the way a dock is a voyage.

Because you are already a forest,
and there are dolphins, and lakes and mountains,
and impossible loves
that will be named Celia.

Alguien dice tu nombre en el futuro
y se llena de gente una casa vacía,
todos se sientan a la mesa.

Ya lo habrás olvidado,
fue la felicidad quien sembró este dolor,
fue la felicidad igual que una tormenta
sobre un vaso vacío.

Cuando lleguen el miedo y la desesperanza,
y todas las cerezas hayan caído al barro,
y las gaviotas griten
el olvido imposible de una mujer herida
que siente que avanzar es quedarse más sola . . .

Si todo esto sucede
recuerda la manera en que la lluvia
se convierte en un árbol
y el modo en que las olas
son el final del agua y el principio del mar.

No conoces el mar, ni el barro, ni los árboles,
pero ya eres un bosque por el que pasa un río.

Someone says your name in the future
and people fill an empty house,
seat themselves at the table.

You will have forgotten it,
it was happiness that sowed this pain,
it was happiness like a storm
above an empty glass.

When fear and desperation come,
and all the cherries have fallen into mud,
and seagulls scream
the impossible oblivion of a wounded woman
who feels that going forward is being even more alone . . .

If all this happens
remember how rain
turns into a tree
and the way waves
are the end of the water and the beginning of the sea.

You know not the sea, nor the mud, nor the trees,
yet you are a forest where a river flows.

LA ORILLA DEL PRECIPICIO

En noches como esta me asomo a un precipicio
para seguir tus pasos encima de las piedras.

El verano en Granada
ha convertido en plomo la inercia de las horas:
siempre correr detrás de una ilusión descalza.

Ha cambiado la vida a paso de tormenta,
no existe aquel lugar en el que te has quedado,
puedo volver la vista,
puedo verte mirando el rompeolas,
piensas que la distancia entre hoy y el futuro
es sólo la ambición de los sueños perdidos.

Yo sé que estás allí,
que ahora miras los barcos detrás de los peñones
y piensas en Van Gogh
y en el hueco que queda
en manos de la incertidumbre.

Empieza a amanecer sobre el Danubio,
los delicados puentes parecen horizontes
por los que cruza el día.
Despierta Budapest y despiertas en ella
como la luz de un faro.
Ya no es una ciudad, es un rincón de ti.

Yo quisiera buscarte por todas las ciudades,
pero siempre regreso
porque en aquella orilla no hay muerte que celebre
el tacto de tu infancia,
o las cosas que nunca sucedieron.

THE EDGE OF THE CLIFF

On nights like this I lean over the cliff
to follow your footsteps on the stones.

Summer in Granada
has turned the inertia of hours to lead:
always chasing a barefoot illusion.

Life has changed quickly as a storm,
the place you stayed no longer exists,
I can look back,
can see you watching the breakwater,
you think the distance between today and the future
is only the ambition of lost dreams.

I know you're there,
that you watch the ships beyond the rocks
and think about Van Gogh
and the empty space that hangs
in the hands of uncertainty.

It begins to dawn over the Danube,
delicate bridges seem like horizons
that this day will cross.
Budapest awakens and you awaken in it
like light from a beacon.
It's no longer a city, it's a corner of you.

I would like to look for you in every city,
but I always come back here
for on that far shore there's no death to celebrate
the touch of your childhood,
or the things that never happened.

UN CAMINO HACIA TI

Igual que los cobardes cuando huyen
van construyendo un rastro,
yo he dejado un camino que conduce hasta ti.

Ahora estás al final
de esos bosques que brotan
de forma inesperada
en el último instante de un adiós,
detrás de cada verso que intenta sostener
el agua en el vacío.

El invierno ha borrado el horizonte,
la nieve que fue el brillo de tus ojos
ha convertido en barro mis certezas.
Dónde correr ahora,
agotado y exhausto,
este dolor de sombras
se pregunta el lugar en el que crecen
los árboles que eligen los ahorcados,
los estanques de la oportunidad.

Cobarde caminante que prefiere
la ciudad de las horas detenidas,
la sombra de los sauces
y el orden de los cuerpos conocidos.

He dejado un camino que conduce hasta ti,
he dejado un camino.

A TRAIL TO YOU

Just the way cowards fleeing
always leave their trace,
I have left a trail that leads to you.

You are at the end
of those woods that sprout up
unexpectedly
in the final moment of a farewell,
behind every verse that would hold
water in a vacuum.

Winter has smudged the horizon,
snow that shined in your eyes
has turned my certainty to mud.
Where to run to now,
worn down and exhausted,
this shadowy grief
makes me wonder where the trees
that hanged men choose grow
like reservoirs of opportunity.

Cowardly wayfarer who prefers
the city of arrested hours,
the shade of willows
and the order of known bodies.

I have left a trail that leads to you,
I have left a trail.

POSTAL DE INVIERNO

Está sola en el mundo y es febrero,
le duelen los pulgares,
se toca la nariz para medir el frío.

Puede ver su reflejo sobre el lago,
los peces melancólicos son ya lunas de octubre
que dibujan sus pasos sobre el hielo.

Allí están los poemas,
en el fondo del lago,
justo un paso detrás de la palabra nunca.

WINTER POSTCARD

She's alone in the world and it's February,
her thumbs ache,
she touches her nose to judge the cold.

She can see her reflection on the lake,
melancholy fish are now October moons
that her steps draw over the ice.

The poems are there,
at the bottom of the lake,
just a step behind the word never.

NOCTURNO DE MALÁ STRANA
(POEMA DE AMOR)

Ha crecido la hierba
en las piedras de esponja del viejo cementerio,
y el olvido,
que levanta sus flores por las enredaderas,
todo lo nombra, en todo se incorpora.

La gente que corría se esconde en los portales
y un silencio de plástico
golpea los carteles y las lápidas.

Las torres grises, agujas de ceniza,
son también la advertencia,
el barro de los ríos,
todo lo que dejé,
las traiciones que ahora me condenan
a esta ciudad de esquinas invisibles,
de llantos que no pueden contenerse,
ya todo el mundo llora el amor que perdí
y el humo se dispersa
y el viento sopla a ráfagas
arrastrando el otoño,
llevándose lo último que quedaba de ti.

MALÁ STRANA NOCTURNE
(LOVE POEM)

Grass has grown up
among porous stones of the old cemetery,
and oblivion,
raising its flowers amid creepers,
names everything, becomes a part of everything.

People who ran away hide in doorways
and a plastic silence
strikes the bulletins and tombstones.

The gray towers, needles of ash,
are also a warning,
the mud of rivers,
everything I left behind,
the treacheries now condemning me
to this city of invisible corners,
of uncontainable grief,
now everyone mourns the love I lost
and smoke dissipates
and the wind blows in gusts
dragging autumn along,
carrying away what was left of you.

MADRUGADA

Así pasa la vida desde que ya no estás,
mostrándome el camino por el que no te has ido.

DAYBREAK

This is how life goes now that you're gone,
showing me the road you didn't take.

MADRUGADA

Hoy quiero la tristeza que siempre te acompaña
y que la vida tenga ese sabor amargo
de los días sin ti.

DAYBREAK

Today I want the sadness that always accompanies you
and I want life to have that bitter taste
of these days without you.

AYER

Ahora que cae noviembre sobre el mar,
las palabras son árboles.

Nadie sabe decirme
si existe tu recuerdo
o es sólo la mitad del infinito,
todo lo que me importa.

YESTERDAY

Now with November falling over the sea,
words are trees.

No one can tell me
if my mcmory of you exists
or is only half of infinity,
everything that matters to me.

EL JUGADOR

Nos jugamos la vida a cara o cruz.
Sé que no va a gustarte,
pero no hemos logrado responder
por qué vale la pena,
qué significa todo,
dónde espera la nada
que está menos presente
pero en todas las cosas.

No vayas a quejarte,
por esta oscuridad han pasado tus dedos
palpando las paredes.

Ya tienes la moneda entre las manos
y no será el azar quien la deslice
ni la suerte su impulso.

Hoy sujetas los días que vendrán
y los lanzas

                                                  y flota

la tristeza en el aire
girando con el vértigo
de lo que pudo ser
otra vida contigo.

THE GAMBLER

We gamble with life, heads or tails.
I know you won't like it,
but we haven't figured out
why it matters,
what it all means,
where nothingness lurks
less present
but in all things.

Don't start complaining,
your fingers have passed through this darkness
feeling the walls.

You have the coin in your hands
and it will not be chance that lets it slip
nor luck its impulse.

Today you hold the days to come
and you flip them

                                        and sadness floats

through the air
spinning with the dizziness
of what could have been
another life with you.

MUELLES ABANDONADOS

Cruza la soledad la muchedumbre
hablando en otro idioma.

Reconozco
el mapa que conduce a las revelaciones.

Imagina las calles de Lisboa,
ignora la distancia inoportuna
con el azar borroso de un deseo dormido,
de esos sueños que son las noches luminosas
y también su añoranza.

Si ahora cierro los ojos
el sol sale en diciembre para tocar tu boca
y tu piel está en mí como un tejado
contiene una ciudad.

Puedo seguir tus pasos por Lisboa,
cambias las estaciones,
eres nieve y arena,
muelles abandonados.

ABANDONED DOCKS

The crowd crosses through the solitude
speaking in another tongue.

I recognize
the map that leads to revelations.

It images the streets of Lisbon,
it ignores inopportune distances
with the random haze of a dormant desire,
of these dreams that are luminous nights
and also their longing.

If I close my eyes now
the sun rises in December to touch your mouth
and your skin is over me the way a rooftop
holds a city.

I can follow your steps through Lisbon,
you change the seasons,
you are snow and sand,
abandoned docks.

La tristeza
en los mapas

La tristeza es anterior al hombre, es la tierra del hombre

LUIS ROSALES

SADNESS
IN MAPS

Sadness came before man, it is the land of man.

LUIS ROSALES

3

(SAN SALVADOR)

Hoy sé que la esperanza
es el miedo
con los ojos vendados.

(SAN SALVADOR)

Today I know that hope
is fear
blindfolded.

(KUTNÁ HORA)

Quiero pensar que todo sigue allí,
porque todo es distinto,
más y más cada vez,
la forma en que envejeces al mirar hacia atrás
y aprendes del fracaso
abrazando la altura y la imprudencia,
la mala suerte,
o el curso de un instante imprevisible.

(KUTNÁ HORA)

I want to think everything is still there,
but it's all different,
more and more every time,
the way you age looking back,
and learn from failure
embracing loftiness and indiscretion,
bad luck,
and the course of an unpredictable moment.

(PUEBLA)

Me acerco a la ventana,
los volcanes se asoman a la tarde
como me asomo ahora a la distancia
que he dejado crecer
entre mi soledad y un barco abandonado.

Pienso que la tristeza
es la tierra del hombre.

(PUEBLA)

I come to the window,
the volcanoes rise into the afternoon
as I rise into the distance
I have allowed to grow
between my loneliness and an abandoned boat.

I think sadness
is the land of man.

(POTOČARI)

Un minuto de sol que sobrevive al musgo,
una oración inmóvil,
un tropiezo en el grito que saca de las rocas
la peor estampida.

Los muertos siempre saben el final del camino.

Los muertos siempre dejan
un silencio apremiante
o los últimos pasos
que convierten a un hombre
en desaparecido.

(POTOČARI)

A moment of sunlight that outlasts moss,
a motionless prayer,
a stutter in the cry that draws from the rocks
the worst stampede.

The dead always know the end of the road.

The dead always leave
an urgent silence
or the final steps
that make a man
disappear.

(BOGOTÁ)

Para Irene

Todas las calles llevan hacia el norte,
allí están las montañas
que vuelcan su misterio en Bogotá
y detienen las horas y el instante
que sujetan tus ojos.

Esta noche en el rostro es el invierno
y es la melancolía que anticipa
una imagen borrosa.

Puedo verlo en el modo en que mantienes
las cosas suspendidas al mirarlas.

Aquella lluvia fina que fue el amanecer
es el agua en mis manos,
las montañas azules son el norte,
todos los mapas buscan un regreso.

(BOGOTÁ)

For Irene

All the streets lead north,
the mountains are there
shrouding Bogotá with their mystery
halting time and the moment
caught in your eyes.

There's winter in your face tonight
and the melancholy promise
of a cloudy image.

I can see it in the way you keep
things suspended in your gaze.

The fine rain at dawn
is the water In my hands,
the blue mountains are the north,
all maps seek a return.

(RUINAS DE TONINÁ, CHIAPAS)

Quiso subir al nido de las águilas
para poder mirar al miedo sin la tierra
y distinguir los días del diluvio.
Entonces vio a lo lejos la quietud infinita,
y vio sobre sí mismo unas raíces
que impedían volar
y de nada sirvió que extendiera los brazos
y sintiera ligeros sus pies encallecidos,
y de nada sirvió que todo el universo
se transformase en niebla,
ni tan siquiera el viento ni su dolor lo pudo.

La muerte siempre lo empujó hacia abajo
y no quiso llorar,
ni lástima ni orgullo quiso llevar con él
al fondo de la tierra.

(RUINS OF TONINÁ, CHIAPAS)

He wanted to climb to the eagles' nest
to see fear without the earth
and to discern the days of deluge.
Then he saw far away infinite calm
and he saw roots growing over him
that kept him from flying
and it was useless to extend his arms
and to feel the lightness of his calloused feet,
and it was useless that the whole universe
turned to fog,
neither the wind nor his grief could handle it.

Death always kept him down
and he did not intend to cry,
nor did he intend to take pity or pride with him
to the bottom of the world.

(LEVIZZANO)

El color que ahora tiene la tarde en los viñedos,
este equilibrio triste
que me recuerda a ti
se ha clavado en los días.

Pero en este poema
has cambiado tu paso de tormenta
por la aceleración,
pasan constelaciones igual que los peldaños
que hay en una escalera.

Los tristes nunca llenan de luz las estaciones
pero miran la luz
con la cadencia lenta del que sabe
lo que dura la noche.

(LEVIZZANO)

The color of afternoon in the vineyards,
this sad balance
that reminds me of you
has nailed itself to each day.

But in this poem
you have left behind your tortuous gait
for speed,
constellations pass by like rungs
on a ladder.

Sad people never fill seasons with light
but they look at light
with the slow cadence of one who knows
how long night lasts.

(PLAZA SINTAGMA, ATENAS)

Puede hacerse real
este desequilibrio,
la carrera suicida de los perros
persiguiendo las motos y los coches,
—su ladrido incesante es la locura—,
el latido del gas,
la desesperación
que es fuego y alambradas,
y también es el miedo
cuando bajas la vista
y caminas con pasos estudiados,
tratando de pasar inadvertido,
como quien busca un sueño que tenga su estatura.

(SYNTAGMA SQUARE, ATHENS)

This imbalance
could become real,
the suicidal dog race
chasing cycles and cars,
—whose incessant barking is madness—,
throbbing exhaust,
desperation
fire and barbed wire,
and also fear
when you lower your eyes
and walk with studied steps,
trying to pass unseen,
like someone seeking a dream just the right size.

(PLAYA DE SAN CRISTÓBAL)

Podéis mirar el mundo a través de mi llanto.

Allí están vuestros cuerpos,
las llaves de un verano suenan en los bolsillos,
alguien llama a la puerta,
el salto de un muchacho es el orgullo,
también la cicatriz sobre el agotamiento,
las rocas que se adentran en el agua.

No he sabido olvidar
y ahora voy a decirte lo que pienso de ti,
precisamente ahora
que ya no te conozco,
porque en este abandono no eres más que un recuerdo
cortado en la tiniebla.

Volví a soñar contigo,
te adentras en el tiempo un poco más,
ya no logro seguirte,
sólo tengo el recuerdo,
he mirado tu cuerpo tantas veces,
tantas veces la sal y la impaciencia,
la forma de tus manos,
el final del pasillo,
el timbre de la puerta
pero nunca eras tú,
seguramente ya no te conozco,
porque en este abandono no eres más que un recuerdo,
el misterio de un hombre frente al propio dolor.

Algo va a suceder,
algo que no ha pasado todavía,

(SAN CRISTÓBAL BEACH)

You can see the world through my grief.

There are your bodies,
the summer keys jingling in your pockets,
someone calls at the door,
a boy's jump is his pride,
as well as the scar on his exhaustion,
rocks leading into the water.

I haven't known how to forget
and now I'm going to tell you what I think of you,
right now
because now I no longer know you,
because in this abandonment you are nothing more than a memory
cut from the dark.

I dreamt of you again,
you retreat a bit more into time,
I can no longer follow you,
I have only the memory,
I have looked at your body so many times,
so many times salt and impatience,
the shape of your hands,
the end of the hall,
the sound of the doorbell
but it was never you,
surely I no longer know you,
because in this abandonment you are no more than a memory,
the mystery of a man facing his pain.

Something is going to happen,
something that hasn't happened yet,

tal vez sea el amor
o tal vez el olvido,
esa sombra que avanza sobre el mundo . . .

No puedo imaginar un mar abandonado.

maybe it will be love
or maybe oblivion,
that shadow advancing over the world . . .

I can't imagine an abandoned sea.

(CAMPO DE LOS MIRLOS)

Es la inercia del odio,
el espanto que corre hacia las balas
y la sangre que crece en manantiales
en los campos del viento.

La ruina de la guerra bebe el amanecer
del mismo modo que los mirlos pueden
ser el fuego que incendia las palabras.

(FIELD OF BLACKBIRDS)

It's the inertia of hatred,
terror running toward bullets
blood spreading through springs
in fields of wind.

The wreckage of war drinks dawn
the way blackbirds could be
fire igniting words.

(AGRA)

Hay un cuerpo tirado entre la muchedumbre.

Poco vale la vida
cuando no queda nada que perder,
apenas un zarpazo,
una herida que sea el prodigio o la grieta,
el pacto de la sangre con el miedo.

(AGRA)

There is a body flung into the multitude.

Life is worth little
when there's nothing left to lose,
hardly a scratch,
a wound perhaps a miracle or perhaps a crack,
the pact of blood with fear.

La luz
no llegará viva
a mañana

A Benjamín Prado

4

THE LIGHT WILL NOT ARRIVE ALIVE TOMORROW

To Benjamín Prado

EL DAÑO

Lo supimos después,
sin tiempo para nada.

Porque tal vez la vida nos dio todo al principio
y seguimos buscando
un camino que lleve a ese lugar,
un puñado de polvo
que guarde el equilibrio suficiente
para no convertirse
en aire o en montaña.

Porque tal vez la vida no nos perteneció
y se fue consumiendo
como todas las cosas que hemos creído nuestras
y son parte del daño
que dibuja las líneas de la historia
derribando ciudades con sus muros.

Y de haberlo sabido
habríamos juntado nuestras manos
o mirado a otra parte.

Y de haberlo sabido,
habríamos mordido nuestros labios
sangrando en el amor
para dejar visibles las heridas,
o habríamos rezado,
o renunciado a todo para quedarnos quietos
y no cruzar los días que agonizan.

Es todo tan inmenso que no cabe en el llanto
y el dolor nos observa desde fuera.

HARM

We found out afterward,
no time for anything.

Because maybe life gave us everything at the start
and we keep on searching for
a road that leads to that place,
a handful of dust
with enough stability
not to turn into
air or a mountain.

Because maybe life didn't belong to us
and went about consuming itself
like all the things we thought were ours,
and they are part of the harm
that draws the lines of history
knocking down cities and their walls.

And had we found out
we would have folded our hands
or looked the other way.

And had we found out
we would have bitten our lips
bleeding in the love
in order to make the wounds visible,
or we would have prayed,
or given up everything to remain still
and not suffer the agony of days to come.

It's all so immense it won't fit into the lament
and grief observes us from afar.

Lo supimos después,
no hay nostalgia más grande que aquella del futuro.

We found out afterwards,
there's no nostalgia greater than that of the future.

LOS RECUERDOS BORRADOS

Al final de la noche,
lejana como infancia o amor desprevenido,
se avista una ciudad.

Brillan sus luces, parpadean,
son faros de otro tiempo,
rostros que no recuerdas pero son familiares,
los brazos fríos,
tu desesperación.

Ahora busco en ellos,
aparece un colegio de monjas junto a un río
y se pueblan tus labios de nombres e intuiciones.
También de un uniforme
y de algún privilegio
que pasó por tu vida como lo hace un extraño.

He aprendido a mirar tu juventud
desde la lejanía,
caminas con un paso muy distinto al de ahora,
eres otra mujer
y tus pasos son largos aunque caigas de nuevo
mientras la vida avanza como madera vieja,
febril artesanía y pintura en las manos,
paciencia de derrota acostumbrada,
y el miedo a la desgracia de tres hijos,
tres veces el abismo.

Conoces un camino que termina en nosotros,
defiendo la verdad de tu intuición,
los jarrones antiguos se llenan de monedas
y objetos inservibles,

MEMORIES ERASED

At the end of night,
distant as childhood or an unexpected love,
a city appears.

Its lights shine and flicker,
beacons of another time,
familiar faces you can't recall,
cold arms,
your desperation.

Now I search through them,
a school with nuns appears beside a river
and your lips are alive with names and intuitions.
And also with a uniform
and a certain privilege
that passed through your life like a stranger.

I have learned to see your youth
from afar,
your walk was quite different than it is now,
you are a different woman
and your steps are long even though you fall again
while life goes on like aging wood,
feverish artistry and paint on your hands,
the patience of accustomed failure,
and fear of the misfortune of three boys,
three times the abyss.

You know a road that ends at us,
I defend the rightness of your intuition,
the ancient urns fill with coins
and useless objects,

pasan por tu memoria como espejos idénticos
el uno frente al otro.

Me duele imaginar la realidad
porque extiendo tu mano por las cosas
y hay un tacto cansado que celebra la vida.

they run through your memory like identical mirrors
one facing the other.

It hurts to imagine reality
how I extend your hand among these things
and there is a worn touch that celebrates life.

EL ÁRBOL DE LA FIEBRE

Todos buscan el árbol de la fiebre,
son legiones de miedo
que vuelcan sus palabras,
que no saben callar,
el silencio es la mano que les cubre los ojos,
la escalera de hielo que baja hasta las aguas,
y no saben callar,
atraviesan los páramos
para juntar sus labios con la lluvia,
han llenado sus bocas de agua y de raíces
y no saben callar,
con un nudo de sangre y el pulso de un enfermo,
las sacudidas lentas que son el equilibrio
y también son la vida derramada,
el tejido inestable que sostiene una arteria.

Llevan en los pulmones insectos y lombrices,
se consumen las horas en los escalofríos
y las sábanas saben a sudor,
son saladas y duelen en los codos.

Ya son la podredumbre
que camina o se arrastra,
que tiene un solo rostro,
la vida en una gota que es la luz
pero también la sombra,
la lengua que es el paso de los pobres,
la lengua que se alarga hasta agotar la sed
como un vaso de angustia.

Ahora que el silencio les rompe las gargantas
el pantano es la forma de la fiebre

THE FEVER TREE

They seek the fever tree,
legions of the fearful
blurting their words,
not knowing how to shut up,
silence the hand that covers their eyes,
the icy stairway leading down to water,
and they don't know how to shut up,
they cross barren plains
press their lips to the rain,
fill their mouths with water and roots
and don't know how to shut up,
with a clot of blood and the pulse of the sick,
the slow shaking is balance
and also the hemorrhaging of life
the unstable tissue sustaining an artery.

They carry insects and worms in their lungs,
waste away the hours in chills
and sheets that smell of sweat,
that are salty and make their elbows hurt.

They are now the putrescence
that walks or drags itself,
that has only one face,
life in a single drop that is light
and also shadow,
the tongue that is the passage of the poor,
the tongue that stretches to the end of thirst
like a glass full of anguish.

Now that silence rends their throats
the bog takes the shape of a fever

y en su orilla los muertos ya no miran
hacia la multitud
que también los ignora
como la boca negra que hay en una serpiente.

Todos buscan el árbol,
todos quieren beber la lluvia de sus hojas,
sólo unos pocos de ellos serán afortunados,
van a aplazar la muerte,
van a cambiar la piel de los pantanos,
el vapor de las ciénagas,
por el hielo que corta los labios en mitades,
por el tiempo que borra los rostros de la carne,
por el fondo del mar.

and on its shores the dead no longer look
to the multitude
that ignores them
like the black mouth inside a snake.

They all seek the tree,
want to drink the rain from its leaves,
only a few will be fortunate,
will stave off death,
will trade the skin of the bogs,
the swamp's steam,
for the ice that slices lips in half,
for time that erases flesh from faces,
for the bottom of the sea.

EL TERREMOTO

A Eden Tosi

La sangre de las ocas que bañaba la tierra
se ha vuelto inexplicable,
hierve como el deseo.
Las cordilleras andan y el horizonte tiene
la apariencia del agua.

En los viñedos,
un temblor bajo el suelo es el insomnio.

Ya no se espera a Dios en este continente,
son viejos los ladrillos y gastados los sueños
como niños con hambre
que habitan los barrancos.

Siento el olor a pólvora debajo de la tierra
y la necesidad de abrazarme a los árboles.

El balcón está abierto,
sobre la cama el techo resulta una amenaza,
basta un golpe certero, una viga que ceda
roída por el beso de la lluvia podrida,
para hacer que el milagro se transforme en dolor.

Es tan simple, tan frágil,
tan vulnerable al fin:
caminan las montañas y vuelcan campanarios
sobre estatuas de bronce y nombres que son huellas
que conducen al miedo.

Hay ventanas que ceden,
sillas que se resbalan,
calles por las que cruza una desgracia.

EARTHQUAKE

To Eden Tosi

The blood of geese that bathed the earth
has become inexplicable,
boils like desire.
Mountain ranges walk and the horizon
looks like water.

In vineyards,
a tremor beneath the ground is insomnia.

No one waits for God on this continent,
bricks are old and dreams worn out
like hungry children
living in ravines.

I smell gunpowder beneath the earth
and need to embrace trees.

The balcony is open,
the ceiling above the bed a threat,
it would only take one accurate blow, for a beam,
eaten away by the kiss of decaying rain, to yield
and turn the miracle to grief.

It's so simple, so fragile,
so vulnerable in the end:
mountains walk and bell towers tumble
over bronze statues and names that are tracks
leading back to fear.

There are windows that give,
chairs that slide,
streets where misfortune crosses.

No estaremos a salvo hasta que hayamos muerto.
Quizá después de todo nos persiga el dolor
como barro pegado en los zapatos.

Se mueven las montañas esta noche cualquiera
y al tropezar calculo la distancia
que existe entre los pies y la felicidad.

We will not be safe until we are dead.
Maybe pain pursues us after all
like mud stuck to our shoes.

The mountains move on this particular night
and as I trip I calculate the distance
between my feet and happiness.

CONVERSIÓN EN SOMBRA

He empezado a notarlo,
en tu forma de andar y en tus silencios,
en el modo en que el viento te acoge cuando pasas
o el golpe de la luz sobre tus párpados
en las horas incómodas.

Sombra que apaga el fuego
cuando todo está a oscuras.

Ahora empiezo a temer los días luminosos,
el descaro continuo de los fuertes,
el recuerdo que estás
dejando como vaho en los cristales.

Se confunden tus pasos
que cruzan la otra orilla del invierno,
ya no puedo alcanzarte,
tu lentitud es firme
y mi velocidad
se estrella contra todo lo que aún no ha existido.

Te vas volviendo sombra
y me tocas los ojos
como tocan los ciegos el aire cuando miran,
y cruzas los pantanos
hasta tu habitación
en el momento menos oportuno
para dejar las cosas en silencio
y ser la soledad
que se ocupa de mí.

BECOMING SHADOW

I've begun to notice it,
in the way you walk and your silences,
in the way wind welcomes you as you pass
or the stroke of light on your eyelids
in difficult moments.

Shadow that puts out the fire
when everything is dark.

Now I begin to fear bright days,
the constant impudence of the strong,
the memory you are
leaving like breath on the windowpanes.

Your steps falter
crossing the far shore of winter,
I can no longer reach you,
your slowness is steady
and my speed
crashes into everything that has not yet existed.

You are turning into shadow
and touch my eyes
the way the blind touch air when they look,
and you cross the morass
to your room
at the least opportune moment
leaving things in silence
to become the solitude
that possesses me.

VIAJE

A Daniela Claribel

Esta noche de insomnio
voy a escribir tu nombre en el cristal
y a mirar las montañas
deshaciéndose igual que los recuerdos.

Aquello que no vuelve no puede envejecer,
no se arrugan sus rostros en vagones mojados.

Hay cosas importantes que quisiera decirte
una
por
una
pero se escurren todas las palabras.
Escribo *Todavía*
y veo caer la nieve sobre el rostro
de quien se sabe solo.

No se puede viajar sobre un recuerdo.

JOURNEY

For Daniela Claribel

In this night of insomnia
I'm going to write your name on the windowpane
and watch mountains
come apart like memories.

What doesn't return cannot age,
their faces won't wrinkle on a damp train.

There are important things I want to tell you
one
by
one
but the words slip.
I write *Yet*
and see snow falling on the face
of one who knows he's alone.

You can't travel on a memory.

SI TODAVÍA EXISTE EL MAR

Ya no existe aquel mar
que fue verde en los ojos,
gaviotas suspirando por el fin de los días
y un balcón.

No puedo renunciar a que las cosas
regresen
y empiezo a parecerme a mis derrotas,
a mis viejos temores del tamaño del mar
que todo lo humedecen,
que son toda certeza y toda duda.

IF THE SEA STILL EXISTS

That sea no longer exists
green in my eyes,
gulls sighing for the end of days
and a balcony.

I can't deny the fact that things
return
and I come to resemble my failures,
my old fears about the size of the sea
that dampened everything,
all certainty and all doubt.

LA DEBILIDAD DE LA LUZ

Es la debilidad que hay en la luz
un principio del fuego.

¿Dónde comienza el fuego?
No el que abrasa nervioso los arbustos,
ni el que riega los campos de ceniza,
me refiero a un incendio que sucede en las sombras
y habita en el futuro desde el llanto.
Para reconocerlo
basta sentir el miedo atroz
que no deja dormir
tras un presentimiento del vacío.

Todo le pertenece,
incluso la nostalgia que llega del pasado
y parece escapar del dominio del tiempo
es carne de su asfixia como serán los ojos
que fueron el amor
y también la esperanza
y toda la piedad
y el canto que espantaba los diluvios
porque el cielo escuchaba.

Nunca dejé de hacerlo,
vinieron esas sombras con tu nombre en sus bocas
y te busqué en las llamas
porque fuiste el incendio
y por eso quemé una casa y las noches
se llenaron de lobos
que no van a morderme
porque saben que van a desparecer conmigo.

THE WEAKNESS OF THE LIGHT

It's the weakness in the light
that is the beginning of the fire.

Where does the fire start?
Not the nervous kind that burns bushes,
nor the kind that showers fields with ash,
but the fire that burns in the shadows
and inhabits the future since the cry.
To recognize it
is to feel the atrocious fear
that won't let you sleep
once you've sensed the void.

Everything belongs to it,
even nostalgia for the past
that seems to escape the realm of time,
it's the flesh of her asphyxiation like eyes
that once were love
and also hope
and all the compassion
and the song that frightened away the floods
because heaven listened.

I never stopped doing it,
those shadows came with your name in their mouths
and I searched for you in the flames
because you were the fire
and so I burned down a house and the nights
filled with wolves
that won't bite
because they know they will vanish along with me.

Este enjambre de luces son las sombras
evitando una noche aún mayor
y no tengo ya fuerzas
ni las ganas de entrar en un atardecer.

This swarm of lights is a shadow
avoiding a greater night
and I no longer have the strength
nor the desire to enter an evening.

BABEL

A Jorge Galán

El eclipse de luna que alumbra la ceguera,
el cáncer que es el musgo devorando el futuro,
el amor que descubre los balcones
y salta hacia el vacío,
el llanto que es principio y que escala en los cuerpos
igual que las burbujas revelan los pantanos.

Toda la muchedumbre,
con su débil memoria sujetada
como ruina durmiente,
sucede al mismo tiempo.

En los huesos del bosque,
en la hondura del fango o en la ciénaga
donde las ranas brillan como ortigas,
crecen los esqueletos sobre animales muertos
que riegan las raíces y son enfermedad,
desfiles de silencio que ahogan los tambores.

Ya ha llegado a su sangre,
el corazón del bosque se envenena
bajo la piel del mono,
la infección es del aire y avanza por el agua,
es pasto en la basura y en los charcos de amianto
que ahora lamen las vacas en Jaipur.

Seiscientos mil pulmones serán aire podrido
en las calles de Delhi,
después serán el fuego y la ceniza,
ascuas sobre los ríos,
restos de carne y muerte que camina hacia el mar
en busca de otras bocas.

BABEL

For Jorge Galán

The lunar eclipse that illuminates blindness,
the cancer that is moss devouring the future,
the love that finds balconies
and vaults into the void,
the plaint that begins and surfaces in the body
the way bubbles reveal a bog.

The multitude,
with its faint and constrained memory
like a dormant ruin,
comes together at once.

In the bones of the forest,
in the depths of mud and morass
where frogs shine like nettles,
grow skeletons from dead animals
that nourish the roots and are illness,
silent ranks the drums drown out.

Now it seeps into their blood,
the forest-heart poisoned
beneath the monkey's hide,
the infection is in the air and spreads through water,
is forage in the garbage and in puddles of asbestos
the Jaipur cows lap up.

Six hundred thousand lungs turn to putrid air
in Delhi's streets,
then turn to fire and ash,
cinders in rivers,
remnants of flesh and death going to sea
in search of other mouths.

Todo sucede al mismo tiempo.

Ella se ha despedido,
su paso es el desorden,
un alfiler templado que atraviesa el asombro
igual que un nadador es un huésped del agua.

La mujer de las horas detenidas
se desploma en el suelo del lavabo.
Los recuerdos se apagan,
son luces que se intuyen en la costa,
farolas encendidas
que dibujan la línea del naufragio.
El cofre de cartón que los guardaba
se vuelve un laberinto,
los trajes entallados se confunden
con zapatillas viejas
y los rostros son puertas de salida,
escaleras que llenan los borrachos,
aceras subterráneas,
curvas que son paredes.

Toda la angustia elige el mismo tiempo.
El diluvio que llena de barro los colchones,
la desembocadura,
su agonía de oro que acaba en los tumultos.

Todo ya es parte de la misma herida.

La noche con sus bordes,
los viajeros que cargan el peso de la luna,
el paisaje nocturno y el relámpago,
la tormenta y el duelo,

It's all happening at once.

She has said goodbye,
a disorderly passing,
a stiff pin puncturing surprise
the way a swimmer is the water's guest.

The woman of stilled moments
slumps to the bathroom floor.
Her memories dim,
lights seen faintly on the coast,
lanterns lit
to sketch a shipwreck.
The cardboard chest that held them
has become a labyrinth,
tailored suits tangled with
old slippers,
and faces are now exit doors,
stairways filled with drunks,
underground sidewalks,
curves that are walls.

All anguish chooses the same moment.
Floods fill mattresses with mud,
water gushes,
its golden agony ending in tumult.

Now it's all part of the same wound.

Night with its edges,
travelers bearing the weight of the moon,
the nocturnal landscape and lightning bolt,
storm and grief,

los amantes que sienten en los labios
un sabor parecido
al último minuto de sol sobre la hierba.

Todo sucede al mismo tiempo,
y se adentra en la niebla,
y se detiene.

lovers who feel on their lips
a taste like
the last minute of sunshine on grass.

It's all happening at once,
and it slips into the fog,
and it waits.

Dedicatorias

DEDICATIONS

DEDICATORIAS

(como quien sigue un rastro sobre sus propias huellas)

Bogotá es de Chus y conchita, de Luis, Almudena y Elisa, pero sobre todo es de Irene bajo una lluvia fina de septiembre. San Salvador son Benjamín y María en la Playa de la Libertad, Roxana Méndez en Los Planes, Buyo en El Tunco, los Fajardo junto a un piano y Raquel Lanseros cruzando la Plaza Cívica con todas las miradas clavadas en ella. Francisco Ruiz Udiel todavía pasea solitario por los soportales de Pátzcuaro. En Chiapas están más cerca del cielo Andrea y Fer Muriel mientras Tito e Irene observan la distancia entre la realidad y sus sombras en San Juan Chamula. Federico y Sebastián Díaz-Granados buscan a Baudelaire bajo la lluvia de París, Nieves da media vuelta y decide entrar en la casa del general en Lazarevo cuando la noche crece. Valle Grande es de Alí Calderón, que me acompañó hasta la última quebrada, que entró conmigo al Hospital de Malta. Dahlonega es de Gordon E. McNeer, que sabe lo que cuestan los recuerdos, que no puede cerrar sus casas. Nueva York es de la princesa palestina, Nathalie Handal, que fue poeta en Andalucía porque tiene en los ojos la huella de Belén. Levizzano es de Andrea Cote al final de un camino que lleva a los viñedos. Villa Aiola es de Eden Tosi, caballero del Ottocento que habita en una partitura de Verdi. Kutná Hora es un banco en el que no se sentó Bianca entre los árboles, pero en donde se detuvo. Almuñécar es el mar abandonado, su balcón imposible es de mi madre y mis abuelos, sus barcos en la orilla de San Cristóbal son de Corina Almagro, María Paz y Cristina Zapico y Miguel Bueno. Lukomir es de quienes llegaron al precipicio, de Carlos Aldazábal que quiso darle

DEDICATIONS

(like someone following a trail of his own footprints)

Bogotá belongs to Chus and Conchita, to Luis, Almudena and Elisa, but above all to Irene under light September rain. San Salvador is about Benjamín and María at Playa de la Libertad, Roxana Méndez in Los Planes, Buyo in El Tunco, the Fajardos next to a piano and Raquel Lanseros crossing the Plaza Cívica with every eye nailed on her. Francisco Ruiz Udiel is still walking alone through the archways in Pátzcuaro. In Chiapas Andrea and Fer Muriel are closer to heaven while Tito and Irene observe the distance between reality and its shadows in San Juan Chamula. Federico and Sebastián Díaz-Granados are looking for Baudelaire under a fine Paris rain. Nieves turns around and decides to enter the house of the General in Lazarevo with night coming on. Valle Grande belongs to Alí Calderón, who accompanied me to the last ravine, who went with me to the Hospital of Malta. Dahlonega belongs to Gordon E. McNeer, who knows the price of memories and can't shutter his houses. Nerja belongs to Allen Josephs, who knows the dramatic beauty of mountains sliding into the sea, who knows the sublime. New York is about the Palestinian princess, Nathalie Handal, who was a poet in Andalucía because she carries the sign of Bethlehem in her eyes. Levizzano belongs to Andrea Cote at the end of a road leading to vineyards. Villa Aiola is about Eden Tosi, a cavalier of the Ottocento who inhabits a score by Vivaldi. Kutná Hora is a bench where Bianca did not sit among the trees, but where she did pause. Almuñécar is the abandoned sea, the impossible balcony is my mother and my grandparents, the boats on the shore of San Cristóbal are

queso a los osos, de Paula Bozalongo, Alberto Pérez . . . Aunque solo sea por algún domingo de Gloria. Babel es para Jorge Galán, porque puede imaginarlo mejor que nadie. El viaje es de Daniela Claribel, porque todos los mapas se guardan en sus ojos. El futuro es de Celia, que crece en Sanlúcar de Barrameda con los Sánchez Pacheco, entre el final del agua y el principio del mar.

Corina Almagro, María Paz and Cristina Zapico and Miguel Bueno. Lukomir is for those who went to the edge of the cliff, for Carlos Aldazábal who wanted to feed cheese to the bears, for Paula Bozalongo, Javier Gutiérrez Lozano and for all those who saw the wound of the past in Sarajevo. In Granada Dani, Javier and Lucía Bozalongo, Alberto Fregenal, José Espinar, Verónica Triviño, Luis Ramírez and Mani Pérez are holding on. Even if it's only on some Easter Sunday. Babel is for Jorge Galán, because he can imagine it better than anyone. The journey is for Daniela Claribel, because she keeps all the maps in her eyes. The future belongs to Celia, who is growing up in Sanlúcar de Barrameda in the Sánchez Pacheco family, between the end of the river and the beginning of the sea.

Fernando Valverde is visiting distinguished professor in the Department of Spanish, Italian, and Portuguese at the University of Virginia. He is the author of several books of poetry, including *Eyes of the Pelican*. He has received some of the most significant awards for poetry in Spanish, including the Federico García Lorca, the Emilio Alarcos del Principado de Asturias, and the Antonio Machado.

A world-renowned Hemingway scholar and past president of the Hemingway Society, Allen Josephs has written a dozen books, including *On Hemingway and Spain*; *White Wall of Spain*; *For Whom the Bell Tolls: Ernest Hemingway's Undiscovered Country*; and *Ritual and Sacrifice in the Corrida*. He is also an authority on Spanish poet Federico García Lorca and has published four critical editions of Lorca's poetry and plays in Spain, as well as *Only Mystery: Federico García Lorca's Poetry in Word and Image*. His latest book is *On Cormac McCarthy: Essays on México, Crime, Hemingway and God*. He is University Research Professor at the University of West Florida, where he has taught for over fifty years.

Laura Juliet Wood, MFA in fiction writing from Columbia University, has had her poems and translations published in numerous journals, including the *Los Angeles Review*, the *Atlanta Review*, and the *West Marin Review*. She is currently teaching poetry for the San Miguel International Writers' Festival and is the author of the books of poems *All Hands Lost* and *Dreaming During the Advent of Rain*. She and her three small children live in San Miguel de Allende, Mexico, and Pensacola, Florida.

CONTEMPORARY SPANISH-LANGUAGE POETRY IN TRANSLATION

Allen Josephs, Series Editor

Sponsored by the University of West Florida

This series presents contemporary Spanish-language poets in a bilingual format. The translations are as faithful to the original as possible in order to facilitate comprehension and retain meaning, introducing students of Spanish and poetry readers alike to the best Spanish-language poetry being written today.

The Insistence of Harm, by Fernando Valverde, translated by Allen Josephs and
    Laura Juliet Wood (2019)